This book
belongs
to

_____

Given to me by

_____

FREE cheetah coloring pages!
Visit here for your free gift:

subscribepage.com/u0f2u8

I LOVE BEING A CHEETAH!

By Merrie Mim

Illustrated by Artyom Ernst

Dedicated to amazing Cheetahs everywhere and all those who love them.

Publisher: Cherished Pages Publishing
Website: www.CherishedPagesPublishing.com

Contact email: info@CherishedPagesPublishing.com

ISBN: 978-0-578-72947-3

Cover design and illustrations by: Artyom Ernst
First printing edition: 2020

I am a cheetah
I live in Africa

Across the vast savannah I survey
Everything wild and African that happens each day

My body's long and lean
My legs are strong & sleek

My elegant tail trails long behind
To balance me for speed
You see, no animal runs faster than me

I feel the wind and sniff the air,
I watch for movement everywhere

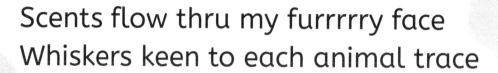

Scents flow thru my furrrrry face
Whiskers keen to each animal trace

impala

blesbok

springbok

thomson's gazelle

grant's gazelle

Hidden by my spotted hair
Silent . . . padding . . . in tall waving grass
Slinking down, down, close to the ground
As Impala and Springbok unknowingly pass

I leap!

And fast! zig zag faster I run!

Stretching my body long to match their dashing rhythm

I chase only what I need,
I am part of the great circle of life
In harmony with other beings

My sound is very small
A mix of chirp and squeak

I clean my face and paws
And purrrrr contentedly
(Do you have a favorite kitty?)

Before you come to Africa
Make a magic wish
To see the
Fastest mammal on earth
A wild African cheetah!

How to love a cheetah

🐾 Make mighty wishes from your heart for the health, happiness and safety of all cheetahs and their families

🐾 Use less plastic so Africa is a healthy place for cheetahs to live

🐾 Pretend you are me! And easily see why I love to be me and love to be free!

Thank you for learning about me by reading this book 🐾

I had wild fun! Hope you did too!

UPCOMING BOOKS
BY
MERRIE MIM

I Love Being a
Camel

I Love Being a
Dog

The Adventures of
Squidget the Clever
Cat Volume 1

The Adventures of
Squidget the Clever
Cat Volume 2

CPSIA information can be obtained
at www.ICGtesting.com
Printed in the USA
LVHW071228161121
703476LV00002B/50